D1105398

Sports Illustrated KIDS

FOR THE RECORD

THE ULTIMATE COLLECTION OF PRO BASEBALL RECORDS

BY ANTHONY WACHOLTZ

CAPSTONE PRESS
a capstone imprint

Sports Illustrated Kids For the Record is published by Capstone Press,
1710 Roe Crest Drive, North Mankato, Minnesota 56003.
www.capstonepub.com

SI Kids is a trademark of Time Inc. Used with permission.

The author dedicates this book to Richard Wacholtz (for his baseball sense)
and Curt Buhl (the biggest die-hard Twins fan he knows).

Library of Congress Cataloging-in-Publication Data
Wacholtz, Anthony.
  The ultimate collection of pro baseball records / by Anthony Wacholtz.
    p. cm.—(Sports illustrated kids. For the record.)
  Includes index.
  ISBN 978-1-4296-8714-0 (library binding)
  ISBN 978-1-4296-9428-5 (paperback)
  1. Baseball—Records—United States—Juvenile literature. I. Title.
  GV877.W335 2013
  796.357'64—dc23   2012016718

Editorial Credits
Catherine Neitge, managing editor; Gene Bentdahl, designer; Eric Gohl, media researcher;
        Eric Manske, production specialist

Photo Credits
AP Images: 45; Corbis: Bettmann, 4–5, 11b; Getty Images: *Sporting News*, 30b; Library of
Congress: 9, 10t, 10b, 11t, 12t, 12b, 13t, 13b, 14b, 17b, 18t, 18b, 21, 23t, 23b, 25, 26t, 26b, 28t,
28b, 33t, 34b, 35m, 35b, 43b, 54b, 58, 60, 61t; Newscom: Icon SMI/Robert Beck, 36, 49t, Icon
SMI/*Sporting News* Archives, 42, Icon SMI/William A Guerro, 47t; Shutterstock: nikkytok,
cover, Tomislav Forgo, back cover (ball), zimmytws, back cover (field); *Sports Illustrated*: Al
Tielemans, 2m, 57t, 57b, Andy Hayt, 55, Bob Rosato, 29b, 48t, Chuck Solomon, 8t, 46, Damian
Strohmeyer, 15, 39t, David E. Klutho, 27, 37t, Heinz Kluetmeier, 19t, 48b, Hy Peskin, 20, 53t,
John Biever, 2b, 8b, 53b, 59, John D. Hanlon, 19b, 50b, John G. Zimmerman, 2t, 24, 29t, 39b,
John Iacono, 3, 22, 31t, 32, 34t, 40, 43t, 44, 56, John W. McDonough, 31b, Manny Millan, 37b,
50t, Mark Kauffman, 17t, Richard Meek, 41b, 51, Robert Beck, 16b, 38, 54t, Simon Bruty, 47b,
Tony Triolo, 30t, 61b, V.J. Lovero, 6, 7b, 33b, 35t, 49b, Walter Iooss Jr., 7t, 14t, 16t, 41t, 52

Design Elements
Shutterstock: ArtyFree, fmua, ssuaphotos, Tomislav Forgo, zimmytws

Printed in the United States of America in North Mankato, Minnesota.
042012   006682CGF12

TABLE OF CONTENTS

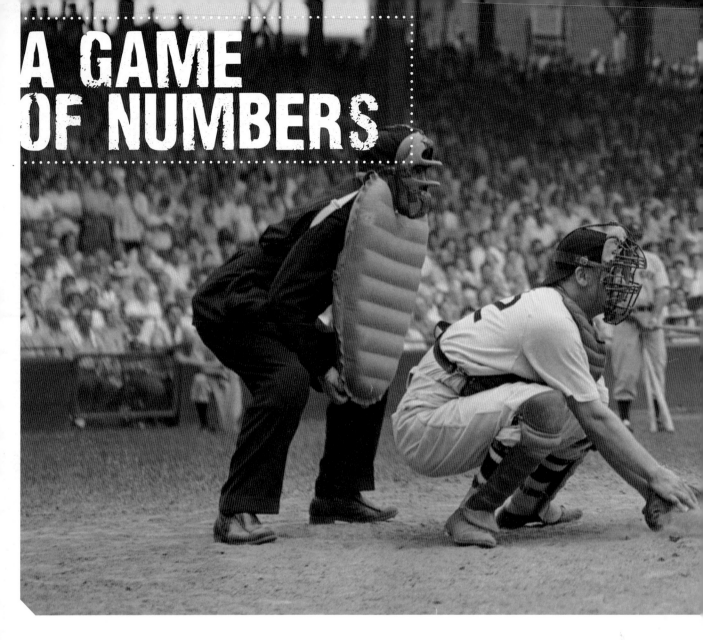

Joe DiMaggio stepped up to the plate for the New York Yankees on May 15, 1941. The cleanup hitter faced Eddie Smith of the Chicago White Sox. DiMaggio laced a single that would be his only hit of the day, and the Yankees lost 13-1. But the game would become a legendary piece of baseball history.

DiMaggio went on to collect at least one hit in game after game after game. He surpassed Willie Keeler's hit streak of 45 games from 1897. But he didn't stop there. He continued his streak until July 17. Facing the Cleveland Indians, DiMaggio went 0-3 with a walk. The remarkable streak ended at 56 games.

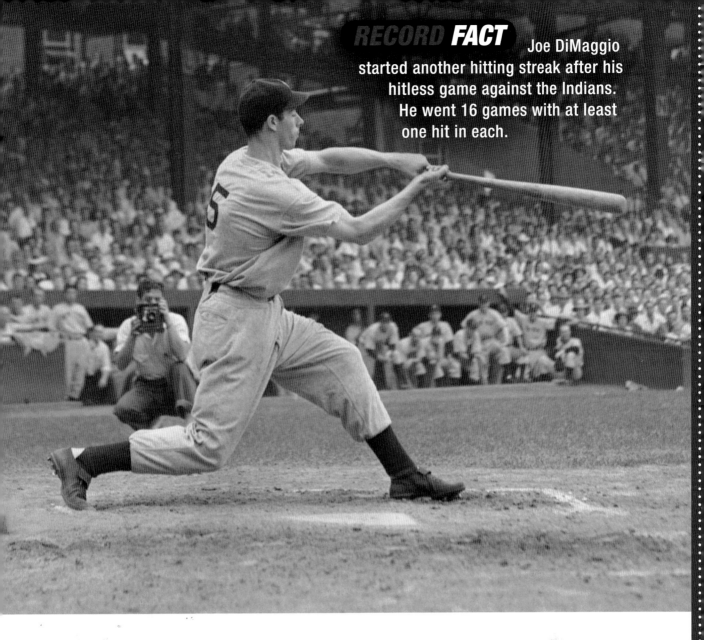

Joe DiMaggio started another hitting streak after his hitless game against the Indians. He went 16 games with at least one hit in each.

More than 70 years later, DiMaggio's streak is still intact. The only person to come close since DiMaggio set the record was the Cincinnati Reds' Pete Rose, who reached 44 games in 1978. Will anyone be able to break DiMaggio's amazing record?

Baseball is filled with records, streaks, and incredible achievements. Players strive to earn a place in baseball history, but it's easier said than done. Once a player gets close to breaking a record, the spotlight shines brightly on him. It's part of what makes baseball such a fun sport to watch. With so many stats, streaks, and records in the game, players will be vying for the top spots on the charts for years to come.

▼ Mark McGwire

CHAPTER 1
HITTING

It's fun to watch a player break any record, but the home run chase is one of the most closely followed records in baseball. In 1961 Roger Maris smashed 61 home runs, passing Babe Ruth's single-season record of 60 set in 1927. Maris' record stood for 38 years.

In 1998 Sammy Sosa and Mark McGwire were on pace to break the record. Although both players surpassed Maris, McGwire was first and ended the season with 70 home runs. Sosa had 66. Only three years later, Barry Bonds notched 73 bombs, a record that still stands.

The 1998 home run chase was an exciting part of MLB history. But it's not just the power hitters who make the record books. Baseball legends Ty Cobb, Pete Rose, and Rickey Henderson weren't known for their power. Instead, they used their hitting ability and speed to enter the record books.

HOME RUNS

HOME RUNS

▼ Hank Aaron

CAREER

1.	Barry Bonds	762	Pirates/Giants	1986–2007
2.	Hank Aaron	755	Braves/Brewers	1954–1976
3.	Babe Ruth	714	Red Sox/Yankees/Braves	1914–1935
4.	Willie Mays	660	Giants/Mets	1951–1952, 1954–1973
5.	Ken Griffey Jr.	630	Mariners/Reds/White Sox	1989–2010
6.	Alex Rodriguez	629	Mariners/Rangers/Yankees	1994–2011*
7.	Sammy Sosa	609	Rangers/White Sox/Cubs/Orioles	1989–2005, 2007
8.	Jim Thome	604	Indians/Phillies/White Sox/Dodgers/Twins	1991–2011*
9.	Frank Robinson	586	Reds/Orioles/Dodgers/Angels/Indians	1956–1976
10.	Mark McGwire	583	Athletics/Cardinals	1986–2001

*Active player

SINGLE SEASON

1.	Barry Bonds	73	Giants	2001
2.	Mark McGwire	70	Cardinals	1998
3.	Sammy Sosa	66	Cubs	1998
4.	Mark McGwire	65	Cardinals	1999
5.	Sammy Sosa	64	Cubs	2001
6.	Sammy Sosa	63	Cubs	1999
7.	Roger Maris	61	Yankees	1961
8.	Babe Ruth	60	Yankees	1927
9.	Babe Ruth	59	Yankees	1921
10.	Four players tied with	58		

▲ Barry Bonds

GRAND SLAMS

▼ Alex Rodriguez

CAREER ||||||||||||||||||||||||||||||||||||||

#	Player		Teams	Years
1.	Lou Gehrig	23	Yankees	1923–1939
2.	Alex Rodriguez	22	Mariners/Rangers/Yankees	1994–2011*
3.	Manny Ramirez	21	Indians/Red Sox/Dodgers/White Sox/Rays	1993–2011*
4.	Eddie Murray	19	Orioles/Dodgers/Mets/Indians/Angels	1977–1997
5.	Willie McCovey	18	Giants/Padres/Athletics	1959–1980
	Robin Ventura	18	White Sox/Mets/Yankees/Dodgers	1989–2004
7.	Jimmie Foxx	17	Athletics/Red Sox/Cubs/Phillies	1925–1945
	Ted Williams	17	Red Sox	1939–1960
9.	Hank Aaron	16	Braves/Brewers	1954–1976
	Dave Kingman	16	Giants/Mets/Padres/Angels/Yankees/Cubs/Athletics	1971–1986
	Carlos Lee	16	White Sox/Brewers/Rangers/Astros	1999–2011*
	Babe Ruth	16	Red Sox/Yankees/Braves	1914–1935

*Active player

SINGLE SEASON |||||||||||||||||||||||||||||||||||||||||||||

#	Player		Team	Year
1.	Travis Hafner	6	Indians	2006
	Don Mattingly	6	Yankees	1987
3.	Ernie Banks	5	Cubs	1955
	Jim Gentile	5	Orioles	1961
	Albert Pujols	5	Cardinals	2009
	Richie Sexson	5	Mariners	2006
7.	Many players tied with	4		

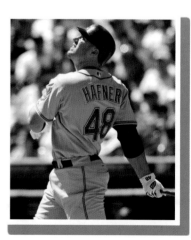
▲ Travis Hafner

RECORD FACT

The St. Louis Cardinals' Fernando Tatis set two eye-opening records April 23, 1999. He became the only player to hit two grand slams in the same inning.

Both home runs came off of Los Angeles Dodgers pitcher Chan Ho Park. The eight RBIs from the two bombs set a record for most RBIs in an inning.

INSIDE-THE-PARK HOME RUNS

CAREER

1.	Jesse Burkett	55	Giants/Spiders/Perfectos/Cardinals/Browns/Americans	1890–1905
2.	Sam Crawford	51	Reds/Tigers	1899–1917
3.	Tommy Leach	48	Colonels/Pirates/Cubs/Reds	1898–1915, 1918
4.	Ty Cobb	46	Tigers/Athletics	1905–1928
	Honus Wagner	46	Colonels/Pirates	1897–1917
6.	Jake Beckley	38	Alleghenys/Burghers/Pirates/Giants/Reds/Cardinals	1893–1907
	Tris Speaker	38	Americans/Red Sox/Indians/Senators/Athletics	1907–1928
8.	Rogers Hornsby	33	Cardinals/Giants/Braves/Cubs/Browns	1915–1937
9.	Edd Roush	31	White Sox/Hoosiers/Pepper/Giants/Reds	1913–1929, 1931
10.	Jake Daubert	30	Superbas/Dodgers/Robins/Reds	1910–1924
	Willie Keeler	30	Giants/Grooms/Orioles/Superbas/Highlanders	1892–1910

▲ Sam Crawford

RECORD FACT

In 1897 Tom McCreery of the Louisville Colonels slammed three in-the-park home runs in a single game.

RUNS BATTED IN

▼ Cap Anson

CAREER

1.	Hank Aaron	2,297	Braves/Brewers	1954–1976
2.	Babe Ruth	2,213	Red Sox/Yankees/Braves	1914–1935
3.	Cap Anson	2,075	Forest Citys/Athletics/White Stockings/Colts	1871–1897
4.	Barry Bonds	1,996	Pirates/Giants	1986–2007
5.	Lou Gehrig	1,995	Yankees	1923–1939
6.	Stan Musial	1,951	Cardinals	1941–1944, 1946–1963
7.	Ty Cobb	1,938	Tigers/Athletics	1905–1928
8.	Jimmie Foxx	1,922	Athletics/Red Sox/Cubs/Phillies	1925–1945
9.	Eddie Murray	1,917	Orioles/Dodgers/Mets/Indians/Angels	1977–1997
10.	Willie Mays	1,903	Giants/Mets	1951–1952, 1954–1973

SINGLE SEASON

1.	Hack Wilson	191	Cubs	1930
2.	Lou Gehrig	184	Yankees	1931
3.	Hank Greenberg	183	Tigers	1937
4.	Jimmie Foxx	175	Red Sox	1938
	Lou Gehrig	175	Yankees	1927
6.	Lou Gehrig	174	Yankees	1930
7.	Babe Ruth	171	Yankees	1921
8.	Hank Greenberg	170	Tigers	1935
	Chuck Klein	170	Phillies	1930
10.	Jimmie Foxx	169	Athletics	1932

▲ Babe Ruth

RUNS BATTED IN

▼ Wilbert Robinson

SINGLE GAME				
1.	Jim Bottomley	12	Cardinals	1924
	Mark Whiten	12	Cardinals	1993
3.	Wilbert Robinson	11	Orioles	1892
	Tony Lazzeri	11	Yankees	1936
	Phil Weintraub	11	Giants	1944
6.	Eight players tied with	10		

HALL OF FAMER JOSH GIBSON

The names of many amazing athletes will never appear in the record books. That's because they weren't allowed to play in the major leagues. Until Jackie Robinson broke baseball's color barrier in 1947, African-Americans played only in the Negro Leagues. Detailed records don't exist to prove it, but hard-hitting catcher Josh Gibson would most likely top many lists. Called the "black Babe Ruth," it is believed that he led the Negro National League in home runs 10 years in a row. Although his career home run total is uncertain, the Baseball Hall of Fame credits him with "almost 800 home runs."

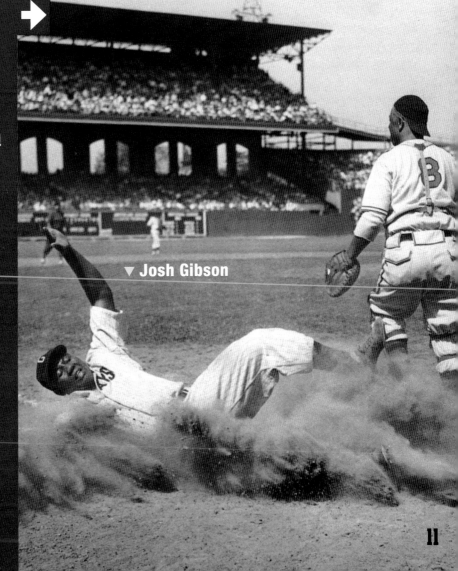
▼ Josh Gibson

RUNS

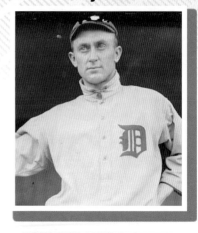

▼ Ty Cobb

CAREER

1.	Rickey Henderson	2,295	Athletics/Yankees/ Blue Jays/Padres/ Angels/Mets/ Mariners/Red Sox/ Dodgers	1979–2003
2.	Ty Cobb	2,246	Tigers/Athletics	1905–1928
3.	Barry Bonds	2,227	Pirates/Giants	1986–2007
4.	Hank Aaron	2,174	Braves/Brewers	1954–1976
	Babe Ruth	2,174	Red Sox/Yankees/ Braves	1914–1935
6.	Pete Rose	2,165	Reds/Phillies/Expos	1963–1986
7.	Willie Mays	2,062	Giants/Mets	1951–1952, 1954–1973
8.	Cap Anson	1,999	Forest Citys/ Athletics/White Stockings/Colts	1871–1897
9.	Stan Musial	1,949	Cardinals	1941–1944, 1946–1963
10.	Lou Gehrig	1,888	Yankees	1923–1939

RECORD FACT

It's hard to get on base six times in one game. But it's even harder to score six times! Only 15 players have scored six runs in a single game. Mel Ott of the New York Giants is the only player to score six times in a game twice in his career.

SINGLE SEASON

1.	Billy Hamilton	198	Phillies	1894
2.	Tom Brown	177	Reds	1891
	Babe Ruth	177	Yankees	1921
4.	Lou Gehrig	167	Yankees	1936
	Tip O'Neill	167	Browns	1887
6.	Billy Hamilton	166	Phillies	1895
7.	Willie Keeler	165	Orioles	1894
	Joe Kelley	165	Orioles	1894
9.	Lou Gehrig	163	Yankees	1931
	Arlie Latham	163	Browns	1887
	Babe Ruth	163	Yankees	1928

▲ Billy Hamilton

BATTING AVERAGE

▼ Joe Jackson

CAREER

1.	Ty Cobb	.366	Tigers/Athletics	1905–1928
2.	Rogers Hornsby	.359	Cardinals/Giants/Braves/Cubs/Browns	1915–1937
3.	Joe Jackson	.356	Athletics/Naps/Indians/White Sox	1908–1920
4.	Lefty O'Doul	.349	Yankees/Red Sox/Giants/Phillies/Robins/Dodgers	1919–1920, 1922–1923, 1928–1934
5.	Ed Delahanty	.346	Quakers/Infants/Phillies/Senators	1888–1903
6.	Tris Speaker	.345	Red Sox/Indians/Senators/Athletics	1907–1928
7.	Billy Hamilton	.344	Cowboys/Phillies/Beaneaters	1888–1901
	Ted Williams	.344	Red Sox	1939–1960
9.	Dan Brouthers	.342	Trojans/Bisons/Wolverines/Beaneaters/Reds/Grooms/Orioles/Colonels/Phillies/Giants	1879–1904
	Babe Ruth	.342	Red Sox/Yankees/Braves	1914–1935

SINGLE SEASON

1.	Hugh Duffy	.440	Beaneaters	1894
2.	Tip O'Neill	.435	Browns	1887
3.	Ross Barnes	.429	White Stockings	1876
4.	Nap Lajoie	.427	Athletics	1901
5.	Willie Keeler	.424	Orioles	1897
	Rogers Hornsby	.424	Cardinals	1924
7.	George Sisler	.420	Browns	1922
	Ty Cobb	.420	Tigers	1911
9.	Tuck Turner	.418	Phillies	1894
10.	Sam Thompson	.415	Phillies	1894

▲ Hugh Duffy

HITS

HITS

▼ Pete Rose

CAREER

1.	Pete Rose	4,256	Reds/Phillies/Expos	1963–1986
2.	Ty Cobb	4,189	Tigers/Athletics	1905–1928
3.	Hank Aaron	3,771	Braves/Brewers	1954–1976
4.	Stan Musial	3,630	Cardinals	1941–1944, 1946–1963
5.	Tris Speaker	3,514	Red Sox/Indians/Senators/Athletics	1907–1928
6.	Cap Anson	3,435	Forest Citys/Athletics/White Stockings/Colts	1871–1897
7.	Honus Wagner	3,420	Colonels/Pirates	1897–1917
8.	Carl Yastrzemski	3,419	Red Sox	1961–1983
9.	Paul Molitor	3,319	Brewers/Blue Jays/Twins	1978–1998
10.	Eddie Collins	3,315	Athletics/White Sox	1906–1930

SINGLE SEASON

1.	Ichiro Suzuki	262	Mariners	2004
2.	George Sisler	257	Browns	1920
3.	Lefty O'Doul	254	Phillies	1929
	Bill Terry	254	Giants	1930
5.	Al Simmons	253	Athletics	1925
6.	Rogers Hornsby	250	Cardinals	1922
	Chuck Klein	250	Phillies	1930
8.	Ty Cobb	248	Tigers	1911
9.	George Sisler	246	Browns	1922
10.	Ichiro Suzuki	242	Mariners	2001

▲ George Sisler

Johnny Burnett of the Cleveland Indians holds the record for most hits in a single game. He pounded out nine hits during a 1932 game, but the game lasted 18 innings. Two players have collected seven hits during a nine-inning game: Wilbert Robinson of the Baltimore Orioles and Rennie Stennett of the Pittsburgh Pirates.

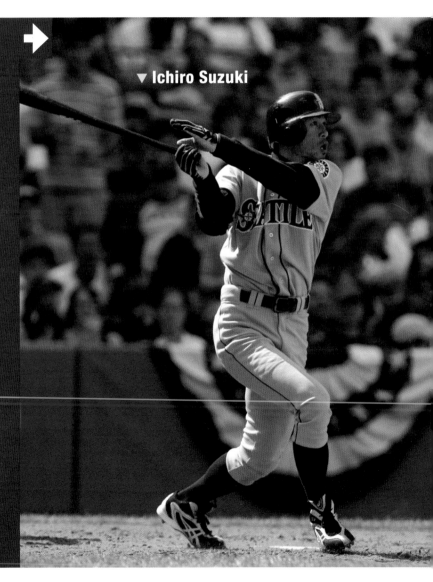

▼ Ichiro Suzuki

WALK AWAY FROM THE WALKS

In 1887 MLB ruled that a player's walks counted toward his hits total. But today those stats don't count on the records lists. For example, Pete Browning and Tip O'Neill each had 275 hits in 1887, which would put them at the top of the single-season hits list. But because walks counted toward their hits total that year, they don't qualify for the top 10. Ichiro Suzuki officially claims the top honor for single-season hits with 262.

SINGLES

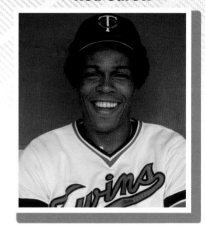

CAREER ||||||||||||||||||||||||||||||||||||||||||||||||||

1.	Pete Rose	3,215	Reds/Phillies/Expos	1963–1986
2.	Ty Cobb	3,053	Tigers/Athletics	1905–1928
3.	Eddie Collins	2,643	Athletics/White Sox	1906–1930
4.	Cap Anson	2,614	Forest Citys/Athletics/White Stockings/Colts	1871–1897
5.	Willie Keeler	2,513	Giants/Grooms/Orioles/Superbas/Highlanders	1892–1910
6.	Honus Wagner	2,424	Colonels/Pirates	1897–1917
7.	Rod Carew	2,404	Twins/Angels	1967–1985
8.	Tris Speaker	2,383	Red Sox/Indians/Senators/Athletics	1907–1928
9.	Tony Gwynn	2,378	Padres	1982–2001
10.	Paul Molitor	2,366	Brewers/Blue Jays/Twins	1978–1998

SINGLE SEASON |||||||||||||||||||||||||||||||||||

1.	Ichiro Suzuki	225	Mariners	2004
2.	Willie Keeler	206	Orioles	1898
3.	Ichiro Suzuki	203	Mariners	2007
4.	Lloyd Waner	198	Pirates	1927
5.	Willie Keeler	193	Orioles	1897
6.	Ichiro Suzuki	192	Mariners	2001
7.	Jesse Burkett	191	Spiders	1896
8.	Willie Keeler	190	Superbas	1899
9.	Wade Boggs	187	Red Sox	1985
10.	Jesse Burkett	186	Spiders	1898
	Ichiro Suzuki	186	Mariners	2006

▲ Ichiro Suzuki

DOUBLES

▼ Stan Musial

CAREER

1.	Tris Speaker	792	Red Sox/Indians/Senators/Athletics	1907–1928
2.	Pete Rose	746	Reds/Phillies/Expos	1963–1986
3.	Stan Musial	725	Cardinals	1941–1944, 1946–1963
4.	Ty Cobb	724	Tigers/Athletics	1905–1928
5.	Craig Biggio	668	Astros	1988–2007
6.	George Brett	665	Royals	1973–1993
7.	Nap Lajoie	657	Phillies/Athletics/Bronchos/Naps	1896–1916
8.	Carl Yastrzemski	646	Red Sox	1961–1983
9.	Honus Wagner	643	Colonels/Pirates	1897–1917
10.	Hank Aaron	624	Braves/Brewers	1954–1976

SINGLE SEASON

1.	Earl Webb	67	Red Sox	1931
2.	George Burns	64	Indians	1926
	Joe Medwick	64	Cardinals	1936
4.	Hank Greenberg	63	Tigers	1934
5.	Paul Waner	62	Pirates	1932
6.	Charlie Gehringer	60	Tigers	1936
7.	Todd Helton	59	Rockies	2000
	Chuck Klein	59	Phillies	1930
	Tris Speaker	59	Indians	1923
10.	Carlos Delgado	57	Blue Jays	2000
	Billy Herman	57	Cubs	1935
	Billy Herman	57	Cubs	1936

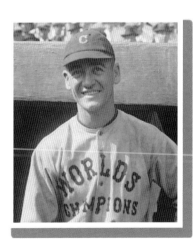

▲ George Burns

TRIPLES

▼ Honus Wagner

CAREER

1.	Sam Crawford	309	Reds/Tigers	1899–1917
2.	Ty Cobb	295	Tigers/Athletics	1905–1928
3.	Honus Wagner	252	Colonels/Pirates	1897–1917
4.	Jake Beckley	244	Alleghenys/Burghers/Pirates/Giants/Reds/Cardinals	1893–1907
5.	Roger Connor	233	Trojans/Gothams/Giants/Phillies/Browns	1880–1897
6.	Tris Speaker	222	Red Sox/Indians/Senators/Athletics	1907–1928
7.	Fred Clarke	220	Colonels/Pirates	1894–1911, 1913–1915
8.	Dan Brouthers	205	Trojans/Bisons/Wolverines/Beaneaters/Reds/Grooms/Orioles/Colonels/Phillies/Giants	1879–1904
9.	Joe Kelley	198	Beaneaters/Pirates/Orioles/Superbas/Reds/Doves	1891–1906
10.	Paul Waner	191	Pirates/Dodgers/Braves/Yankees	1926–1945

SINGLE SEASON

1.	Chief Wilson	36	Pirates	1912
2.	Dave Orr	31	Metropolitans	1886
	Heinie Reitz	31	Orioles	1894
4.	Perry Werden	29	Browns	1893
5.	Harry Davis	28	Pirates	1897
	Sam Thompson	28	Phillies	1894
7.	George Davis	27	Giants	1893
8.	Five players tied with	26		

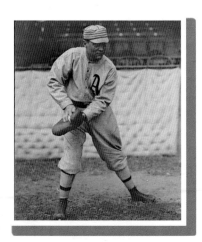

▲ Harry Davis

STOLEN BASES

CAREER

1.	Rickey Henderson	1,406	Athletics/Yankees/Blue Jays/Padres/Angels/Mets/Mariners/Red Sox/Dodgers	1979–2003
2.	Lou Brock	938	Cubs/Cardinals	1961–1979
3.	Billy Hamilton	914	Cowboys/Phillies/Beaneaters	1888–1901
4.	Ty Cobb	897	Tigers/Athletics	1905–1928
5.	Tim Raines	808	Expos/White Sox/Yankees/Athletics/Orioles/Marlins	1979–1999, 2001–2002
6.	Vince Coleman	752	Cardinals/Mets/Royals/Mariners/Reds/Tigers	1985–1997
7.	Arlie Latham	742	Bisons/Browns/Pirates/Reds/Senators/Giants	1880, 1883–1896, 1899, 1909
8.	Eddie Collins	741	Athletics/White Sox	1906–1930
9.	Max Carey	738	Pirates/Robins	1910–1929
10.	Honus Wagner	723	Colonels/Pirates	1897–1917

SINGLE SEASON

1.	Hugh Nicol	138	Red Stockings	1887
2.	Rickey Henderson	130	Athletics	1982
3.	Arlie Latham	129	Browns	1887
4.	Lou Brock	118	Cardinals	1974
5.	Charlie Comiskey	117	Browns	1887
6.	Billy Hamilton	111	Cowboys	1889
	Billy Hamilton	111	Phillies	1891
	Monte Ward	111	Giants	1887
9.	Vince Coleman	110	Cardinals	1985
10.	Vince Coleman	109	Cardinals	1987

▲ Lou Brock

WALKS

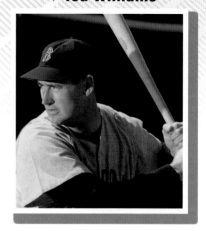

CAREER

1.	Barry Bonds	2,558	Pirates/Giants	1986–2007
2.	Rickey Henderson	2,190	Athletics/Yankees/ Blue Jays/Padres/ Angels/Mets/ Mariners/Red Sox/ Dodgers	1979–2003
3.	Babe Ruth	2,062	Red Sox/Yankees/ Braves	1914–1935
4.	Ted Williams	2,021	Red Sox	1939–1960
5.	Joe Morgan	1,865	Colt .45s/Astros/ Reds/Giants/ Phillies/Athletics	1963–1984
6.	Carl Yastrzemski	1,845	Red Sox	1961–1983
7.	Mickey Mantle	1,733	Yankees	1951–1968
8.	Jim Thome	1,725	Indians/Phillies/ White Sox/ Dodgers/Twins	1991–2011*
9.	Mel Ott	1,708	Giants	1926–1947
10.	Frank Thomas	1,667	White Sox/ Athletics/Blue Jays	1990–2008

*Active player

SINGLE SEASON

1.	Barry Bonds	232	Giants	2004
2.	Barry Bonds	198	Giants	2002
3.	Barry Bonds	177	Giants	2005
4.	Babe Ruth	170	Yankees	1923
5.	Mark McGwire	162	Cardinals	1998
	Ted Williams	162	Red Sox	1947
	Ted Williams	162	Red Sox	1949
8.	Ted Williams	156	Red Sox	1946
9.	Barry Bonds	151	Giants	1996
	Eddie Yost	151	Senators	1956

RECORD FACT

When it comes to intentional walks, Barry Bonds is the king. Pitchers often avoided the slugger's mighty swing by giving him a free ride to first base. Bonds tops the list with 688 career intentional walks. Hank Aaron comes in second with 293—less than half of Bonds' total. In 2004 Bonds was intentionally walked 120 times, which was about one in five plate appearances.

HIT BY PITCH

CAREER ||||||||||||||||||||||||||||||||||||||||

1.	Hughie Jennings	287	Colonels/Orioles/Superbas/Phillies/Tigers	1891–1903, 1907, 1909–1910, 1912, 1918
2.	Craig Biggio	285	Astros	1988–2007
3.	Tommy Tucker	272	Orioles/Beaneaters/Senators/Bridegrooms/Browns/Spiders	1887–1899
4.	Don Baylor	267	Orioles/Athletics/Angels/Yankees/Red Sox/Twins	1970–1988
5.	Jason Kendall	254	Pirates/Athletics/Cubs/Brewers/Royals	1996–2010
6.	Ron Hunt	243	Mets/Dodgers/Giants/Expos/Cardinals	1963–1974
7.	Dan McGann	230	Beaneaters/Orioles/Superbas/Senators/Cardinals/Giants/Doves	1896, 1898–1908
8.	Frank Robinson	198	Redlegs/Reds/Orioles/Dodgers/Angels/Indians	1956–1976
9.	Minnie Minoso	192	Indians/White Sox/Cardinals/Senators	1949, 1951–1964, 1976, 1980
10.	Jake Beckley	183	Alleghenys/Burghers/Pirates/Giants/Reds/Cardinals	1888–1907

RECORD FACT Only two players have been hit by a pitch 50 or more times in one season. Hughie Jennings of the Baltimore Orioles was plunked 51 times in 1896. Seventy-five years later, the Montreal Expos' Ron Hunt was hit by 50 pitches. It must have been an unlucky season for Hunt—his next highest single-season total was 26.

CHAPTER 2

PITCHING

▼ Orel Hershiser

The Los Angeles Dodgers were firmly atop the NL West in September 1988. Their ace, Orel Hershiser, took the mound September 5 to face the Atlanta Braves. Nine dominant innings later, Hershiser had shut out the Braves for the complete game. Notch another win on his belt, and the Dodgers were one step closer to the playoffs.

Hershiser took the mound again September 10, and he pulled off another shutout, this time against the Cincinnati Reds. He followed up the performance with shutouts against the Atlanta Braves, Houston Astros, and San Francisco Giants. By the time he stepped onto the mound against the San Diego Padres September 28, he had pitched 49 consecutive scoreless innings. (He started the streak August 30 when he pitched four scoreless innings against the Montreal Expos.)

All eyes were on Hershiser as he continued to put zeroes on the scoreboard. Each scoreless inning brought him closer to Don Drysdale's streak of 58.2 innings. By the end of the ninth inning, Hershiser's streak reached 58 innings. But the game wasn't over. Tied 0-0, it went into extra innings, and Hershiser stayed in the game. He completed the 10th inning without giving up a run, and the record was his—59 consecutive scoreless innings.

⚾ WINS

CAREER ||||||||||||||||||||||||||||||||||||||||||||||||||||

#	Name	Wins	Teams	Years
1.	Cy Young	511	Spiders/Perfectos/Cardinals/Americans/Naps/Rustlers	1890–1911
2.	Walter Johnson	417	Senators	1907–1927
3.	Grover Alexander	373	Phillies/Cubs/Cardinals	1911–1930
	Christy Mathewson	373	Giants/Reds	1900–1916
5.	Pud Galvin	365	Brown Stockings/Bisons/Alleghenys/Burghers/Pirates/Browns	1875, 1879–1892
6.	Warren Spahn	363	Braves/Mets/Giants	1942, 1946–1965
7.	Kid Nichols	361	Beaneaters/Cardinals/Phillies	1890–1901, 1904–1906
8.	Greg Maddux	355	Cubs/Braves/Dodgers/Padres	1986–2008
9.	Roger Clemens	354	Red Sox/Blue Jays/Yankees/Astros	1984–2007
10.	Tim Keefe	342	Trojans/Metropolitans/Giants/Phillies	1880–1993

SINGLE SEASON ||||||||||||||||||||||||||||||||||||||||||||

#	Name	Wins	Team	Year
1.	Charles Radbourn	59	Grays	1884
2.	John Clarkson	53	White Stockings	1885
3.	Guy Hecker	52	Eclipse	1884
4.	John Clarkson	49	Beaneaters	1889
5.	Charlie Buffinton	48	Beaneaters	1884
	Charles Radbourn	48	Grays	1883
7.	Al Spalding	47	White Stockings	1876
	Monte Ward	47	Grays	1879
9.	Pud Galvin	46	Bisons	1883
	Pud Galvin	46	Bisons	1884
	Matt Kilroy	46	Orioles	1887

▲ John Clarkson

STRIKEOUTS

CAREER

1.	Nolan Ryan	5,714	Mets/Angels/Astros/Rangers	1966, 1968–1993
2.	Randy Johnson	4,875	Expos/Mariners/Astros/Diamondbacks/ Yankees/Giants	1988–2009
3.	Roger Clemens	4,672	Red Sox/Blue Jays/Yankees/Astros	1984–2007
4.	Steve Carlton	4,136	Cardinals/Phillies/Giants/White Sox/ Indians/Twins	1965–1988
5.	Bert Blyleven	3,701	Twins/Rangers/Pirates/Indians/Angels	1970–1990, 1992
6.	Tom Seaver	3,640	Mets/Reds/White Sox/Red Sox	1967–1986
7.	Don Sutton	3,574	Dodgers/Astros/Brewers/Athletics/Angels	1966–1988
8.	Gaylord Perry	3,534	Giants/Indians/Rangers/Padres/Yankees/ Braves/Mariners/Royals	1962–1983
9.	Walter Johnson	3,509	Senators	1907–1927
10.	Greg Maddux	3,371	Cubs/Braves/Dodgers/Padres	1986–2008

SINGLE SEASON

1.	Matt Kilroy	513	Orioles	1886
2.	Toad Ramsey	499	Colonels	1886
3.	Hugh Daily	483	Chicago/Pittsburgh/ Nationals	1884
4.	Dupee Shaw	451	Wolverines/Reds	1884
5.	Charles Radbourn	441	Grays	1884
6.	Charlie Buffinton	417	Beaneaters	1884
7.	Guy Hecker	385	Eclipse	1884
8.	Nolan Ryan	383	Angels	1973
9.	Sandy Koufax	382	Dodgers	1965
10.	Bill Sweeney	374	Monumentals	1884

▲ Sandy Koufax

INNINGS PITCHED

1.	Cy Young	7,356	Spiders/Perfectos/Cardinals/Americans/Naps/Rustlers	1890–1911
2.	Pud Galvin	6,003.1	Brown Stockings/Bisons/Alleghenys/Burghers/Pirates/Browns	1875, 1879–1892
3.	Walter Johnson	5,914.1	Senators	1907–1927
4.	Phil Niekro	5,404	Braves/Yankees/Indians/Blue Jays	1964–1987
5.	Nolan Ryan	5,386	Mets/Angels/Astros/Rangers	1966, 1968–1993
6.	Gaylord Perry	5,350	Giants/Indians/Rangers/Padres/Yankees/Mariners/Royals	1962–1983
7.	Don Sutton	5,282.1	Dodgers/Astros/Brewers/Athletics/Angels	1966–1988
8.	Warren Spahn	5,243.2	Braves/Mets/Giants	1942, 1946–1965
9.	Steve Carlton	5,217.2	Cardinals/Phillies/Giants/White Sox/Indians/Twins	1965–1988
10.	Grover Alexander	5,190	Phillies/Cubs/Cardinals	1911–1930

1.	Will White	680.0	Reds	1879
2.	Charles Radbourn	678.2	Grays	1884
3.	Guy Hecker	670.2	Eclipse	1884
4.	Jim McCormick	657.2	Blues	1880
5.	Pud Galvin	656.1	Bisons	1883
6.	Pud Galvin	636.1	Bisons	1884
7.	Charles Radbourn	632.1	Grays	1883
8.	John Clarkson	623.0	White Stockings	1885
9.	Jim Devlin	622.0	Grays	1876
	Bill Hutchinson	622.0	Colts	1892

▲ Jim McCormick

EARNED RUN AVERAGE (ERA)

CARERER

1.	Ed Walsh	1.82	White Sox/Braves	1904–1917
2.	Addie Joss	1.89	Bronchos/Naps	1902–1910
3.	Jim Devlin	1.90	White Stockings/Grays	1875–1877
4.	Jack Pfiester	2.02	Pirates/Cubs	1903–1904, 1906–1911
5.	Joe Wood	2.03	Red Sox/Indians	1908–1915, 1917, 1919–1920
6.	Mordecai Brown	2.06	Cardinals/Cubs/Reds/Terriers/Tip-Tops/Whales	1903–1916
7.	Monte Ward	2.10	Grays/Gothams	1878–1884
8.	Christy Mathewson	2.13	Giants/Reds	1900–1916
	Al Spalding	2.13	Red Stockings/White Stockings	1871–1877
10.	Tommy Bond	2.14	Atlantics/Dark Blues/Red Stockings/Ruby Legs/Reds/Hoosiers	1874–1882, 1884

SINGLE SEASON

1.	Tim Keefe	0.86	Trojans	1880
2.	Dutch Leonard	0.96	Red Sox	1914
3.	Mordecai Brown	1.04	Cubs	1906
4.	Bob Gibson	1.12	Cardinals	1968
5.	Christy Mathewson	1.14	Giants	1909
	Walter Johnson	1.14	Senators	1913
7.	Jack Pfiester	1.15	Cubs	1907
8.	Addie Joss	1.16	Naps	1908
9.	Carl Lundgren	1.17	Cubs	1907
10.	Denny Driscoll	1.21	Alleghenys	1882

▲ Tim Keefe

▼ Randy Johnson

PERFECT PITCHERS

Any pitcher would be happy to go nine innings without allowing a run for a shutout. To not give up any hits over those nine innings would be even more impressive. But to throw a perfect game—not allowing any hits, walks, errors, or hit batters—is a rare accomplishment. Only 21 players have thrown perfect games in the majors. The youngest pitcher to pull off a perfect game was 20-year-old John Ward for the Providence Grays in 1880. The oldest was Randy Johnson, who completed a perfect game for the Arizona Diamondbacks in 2004 at age 40.

RECORD FACT Chicago White Sox pitcher Mark Buehrle set a pitching record in 2009. He retired 45 batters in a row, breaking the previous record of 41.

SHUTOUTS

CAREGER

1.	Walter Johnson	110	Senators	1907–1927
2.	Grover Alexander	90	Phillies/Cubs/Cardinals	1911–1930
3.	Christy Mathewson	79	Giants/Reds	1900–1916
4.	Cy Young	76	Spiders/Perfectos/Cardinals/Americans/Naps/Rustlers	1890–1911
5.	Eddie Plank	69	Athletics/Terriers/Browns	1901–1917
6.	Warren Spahn	63	Braves/Mets/Giants	1942, 1946–1965
7.	Nolan Ryan	61	Mets/Angels/Astros/Rangers	1966, 1968–1993
	Tom Seaver	61	Mets/Reds/White Sox/Red Sox	1967–1986
9.	Bert Blyleven	60	Twins/Rangers/Pirates/Indians/Angels	1970–1990, 1992
10.	Don Sutton	58	Dodgers/Astros/Brewers/Athletics/Angels	1966–1988

▼ Walter Johnson

SINGLE SEASON

1.	Grover Alexander	16	Phillies	1916
	George Bradley	16	Brown Stockings	1876
3.	Jack Coombs	13	Athletics	1910
	Bob Gibson	13	Cardinals	1968
5.	Grover Alexander	12	Phillies	1915
	Pud Galvin	12	Bisons	1884
	Ed Morris	12	Alleghenys	1886
8.	Eight players tied with	11		

▲ Grover Alexander

SHUTOUTS

CONSECUTIVE SHUTOUT INNINGS PITCHED

1.	Orel Hershiser	59.0	Dodgers	1988
2.	Don Drysdale	58.2	Dodgers	1968
3.	Walter Johnson	55.2	Senators	1913
4.	Jack Coombs	53.0	Athletics	1910
5.	Bob Gibson	47.0	Cardinals	1968
6.	Carl Hubbell	45.1	Giants	1933
7.	Cy Young	45.0	Americans	1904
	Doc White	45.0	White Sox	1904
	Sal Maglie	45.0	Giants	1950
10.	Ed Reulbach	44.0	Cubs	1908

▼ Kerry Wood

STRIKEOUT ACES

Only four pitchers in MLB history have struck out at least 20 batters in a single game. Tom Cheney sent 21 batters back to the dugout over 16 innings in 1962. In 1986 Roger Clemens struck out 20 batters, then repeated the feat 10 years later. In only his fifth major league game, Kerry Wood mowed down 20 hitters in a one-hit masterpiece in 1998. In 2001 Randy Johnson struck out 20 batters over nine innings, but he was replaced when the game went to extra innings.

RECORD FACT

Nolan Ryan is not just the strikeout king. He is also firmly atop the no-hitter records list with seven. The no-hitters occurred during an 18-year span with three teams: the California Angels, Houston Astros, and Texas Rangers.

CY YOUNG WINNERS

Cy Young, the all-time wins leader, had an award named after him in 1956. The annual award honors the two best pitchers, one from the American League and one from the National League.

LEADERS ||||||||||||||||||||

1.	Roger Clemens	7
2.	Randy Johnson	5
3.	Steve Carlton	4
	Greg Maddux	4
5.	Sandy Koufax	3
	Pedro Martinez	3
	Jim Palmer	3
	Tom Seaver	3
9.	Many players tied with	2

▲ Roger Clemens

RECORD FACT   In 1985 Dwight Gooden became the youngest pitcher to win the Cy Young award. The 20-year-old hurler collected 268 strikeouts and eight shutouts that season.

NO RELIEF NEEDED

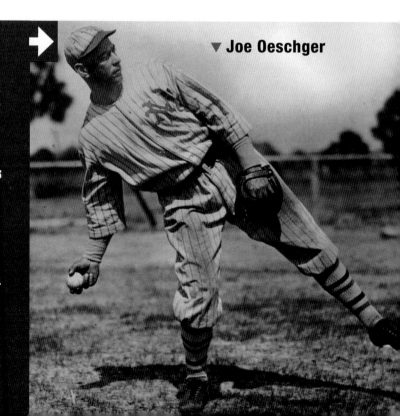

▼ Joe Oeschger

Two players have pitched 26 innings in a single game: Leon Cadore of the Brooklyn Robins and Joe Oeschger of the Boston Braves. The pitchers squared off May 1, 1920. The Robins scored in the top of the fifth, but the Braves tied it up in the bottom of the sixth. Then Cadore and Oeschger matched each other scoreless inning after scoreless inning. After the 26th inning, the game was declared a tie. The 26-inning marathon ranks as the longest game in MLB history.

SAVES

CAREER ||||||||||||||||||||||||||||||||||||||||||||

1.	Mariano Rivera	603	Yankees	1995–2011*
2.	Trevor Hoffman	601	Marlins/Padres/Brewers	1993–2010
3.	Lee Smith	478	Cubs/Red Sox/Cardinals/Yankees/Orioles/Angels/Reds/Expos	1980–1997
4.	John Franco	424	Reds/Mets/Astros	1984–2001, 2003–2005
5.	Billy Wagner	422	Astros/Phillies/Mets/Red Sox/Braves	1995–2010
6.	Dennis Eckersley	390	Indians/Red Sox/Cubs/Athletics/Cardinals	1975–1998
7.	Jeff Reardon	367	Mets/Expos/Twins/Red Sox/Braves/Reds/Yankees	1979–1994
8.	Troy Percival	358	Angels/Tigers/Cardinals/Rays	1995–2005, 2007–2009
9.	Randy Myers	347	Mets/Reds/Padres/Cubs/Orioles/Blue Jays	1985–1998
10.	Rollie Fingers	341	Athletics/Padres/Brewers	1968–1982, 1984–1985

*Active player

SINGLE SEASON ||||||||||||||||||||||||||||||||||||||||||

1.	Francisco Rodriguez	62	Angels	2008
2.	Bobby Thigpen	57	White Sox	1990
3.	Eric Gagne	55	Dodgers	2003
	John Smoltz	55	Braves	2002
5.	Trevor Hoffman	53	Padres	1998
	Randy Myers	53	Cubs	1993
	Mariano Rivera	53	Yankees	2004
8.	Eric Gagne	52	Dodgers	2002
9.	Rod Beck	51	Cubs	1998
	Dennis Eckersley	51	Athletics	1992

▲ Francisco Rodriguez

CHAPTER 3

TEAMS

▼ Alex Rodriguez of the New York Yankees

Most teams go through the highs of winning and the lows of defeat. But every now and then a franchise goes through such an amazing period of success that it becomes known as a dynasty.

The New York Yankees have experienced several dynasties in team history. From Babe Ruth and Lou Gehrig to Derek Jeter and Alex Rodriguez, the team has boasted its fair share of baseball greats. The Yankees definitely know how to win.

It might seem strange to compare the Yankees to the Chicago Cubs—a franchise that hasn't won a World Series in more than 100 years. But many sports experts say that the 1906 Cubs were part of one of baseball's greatest teams. Although they lost the World Series that year, they bounced back to win the championship in 1907 and 1908. Their 116–36 record in 1906 still stands as the best single-season team winning percentage.

WIN-LOSS PERCENTAGE

▼ Babe Ruth of the Yankees & John McGraw of the Giants

BEST (FRANCHISE HISTORY) ||||||||||||||||||||||||||||||

1.	New York Yankees	56.8%	9,767–7,426
2.	San Francisco Giants	53.8%	10,522–9,034
3.	Los Angeles Dodgers	52.4%	10,217–9,278
4.	Boston Red Sox	51.8%	8,909–8,305
	St. Louis Cardinals	51.8%	10,195–9,490
6.	Chicago Cubs	51.3%	10,311–9,779
7.	Cleveland Indians	50.9%	8,771–8,449
8.	Cincinnati Reds	50.7%	9,994–9,702
	Detroit Tigers	50.7%	8,740–8,504
10.	Chicago White Sox	50.6%	8,707–8,496

BEST (SINGLE SEASON) ||||||||||||||||||||||||||||||

1.	Chicago Cubs	76.3%	1906	116–36
2.	Pittsburgh Pirates	74.1%	1902	103–36
3.	Chicago White Stockings	72.6%	1886	90–34
4.	Pittsburgh Pirates	72.4%	1909	110–42
5.	Cleveland Indians	72.1%	1954	111–43
6.	Seattle Mariners	71.6%	2001	116–46
7.	New York Yankees	71.4%	1927	110–44
8.	Detroit Wolverines	70.7%	1886	87–36
9.	Boston Beaneaters	70.5%	1897	93–39
10.	Chicago Cubs	70.4%	1907	107–45

▲ Brett Boone of the Seattle Mariners

RECORD FACT Ties were common in baseball games in the early 1900s. Since ties are not considered wins or losses, they don't count toward a team's win-loss record.

WIN-LOSS PERCENTAGE

WORST (FRANCHISE HISTORY)			
1.	Tampa Bay Rays	44.7%	1,013–1,252
2.	San Diego Padres	46.3%	3,169–3,671
3.	Seattle Mariners	46.7%	2,589–2,956
4.	Philadelphia Phillies	47.3%	9,237–10,292
5.	Baltimore Orioles	47.4%	8,148–9,052
	Texas Rangers	47.4%	3,843–4,272
7.	Washington Nationals	47.5%	3,247–3,583
8.	Colorado Rockies	47.6%	1,437–1,579
9.	Florida Marlins	47.7%	1,435–1,575
	Milwaukee Brewers	47.7%	3,262–3,571

WORST (SINGLE SEASON)				
1.	Cleveland Spiders	13.0%	1899	20–134
2.	Pittsburgh Alleghenys	16.9%	1890	23–113
3.	Philadelphia Athletics	23.5%	1916	36–117
4.	Boston Braves	24.8%	1935	38–115
5.	New York Mets	25.0%	1962	40–120
6.	Washington Senators	25.2%	1904	38–113
7.	Philadelphia Athletics	25.7%	1919	36–104
8.	St. Louis Browns	26.0%	1898	39–111
9.	Detroit Tigers	26.5%	2003	43–119
10.	Pittsburgh Pirates	27.3%	1952	42–112

▲ Guy Hecker of the
Pittsburgh Alleghenys

RECORD FACT Between 1999 and 2001, the Cincinnati Reds went 208 straight games without being shut out.

STREAKS

WINS		
1. New York Giants	26	1916
2. Chicago White Stockings	21	1880
Chicago Cubs	21	1935
4. Providence Grays	20	1884
Oakland Athletics	20	2002
St. Louis Maroons	20	1884

LOSSES		
1. Louisville Colonels	26	1889
2. Cleveland Spiders	24	1899
3. Pittsburgh Alleghenys	23	1890
Philadelphia Phillies	23	1961
5. Philadelphia Athletics	22	1890

▼ Tim Hudson of the Oakland Athletics

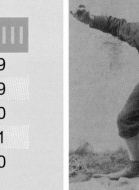

▲ Paul Cook of the Louisville Colonels

A TIE ISN'T A LOSS

The New York Giants hold the record for the longest winning streak in MLB history. But their 26-game streak spanned 27 games. After winning the first 12 games, they tied the Pittsburgh Pirates. Then they won the next 14 games before losing to the Boston Braves.

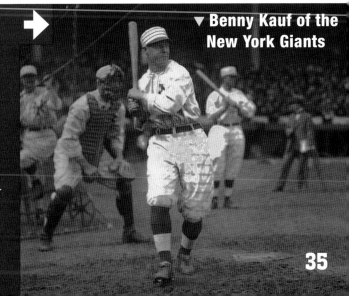

▼ Benny Kauf of the New York Giants

Most runs scored in an inning	18	Chicago White Stockings	1883
Most runs scored in a game	36	Chicago Colts	1897
Most runs scored in a game, both teams	49	Chicago Cubs and Philadelphia Phillies	1922
Most runs scored in a season	1,220	Boston Beaneaters	1894
Most hits in a game	33	Cleveland Indians	1932
Most hits in a season	1,783	Philadelphia Phillies	1930
Most home runs in a game	10	Toronto Blue Jays	1987
Most home runs in a season	264	Seattle Mariners	1997
Most strikeouts in a season	1,529	Arizona Diamondbacks	2010
Lowest ERA in a season	1.73	Chicago Cubs	1907

SLOW START

The Baltimore Orioles had a 21-game losing streak in 1988. That's a tough stretch of games, but it doesn't make the top five for longest losing streaks. However, the first loss of the Orioles' streak came on Opening Day. Almost a full month passed before they won their first game. They hold the unflattering record for worst start to a season.

▼ Eddie Murray

RECORD FACT The Detroit Tigers and Chicago White Sox have combined for the most home runs in a game—twice! The two teams hammered out 12 home runs May 28, 1995, with the Tigers sending out seven. They repeated the feat July 2, 2002, with both teams pounding out six homers.

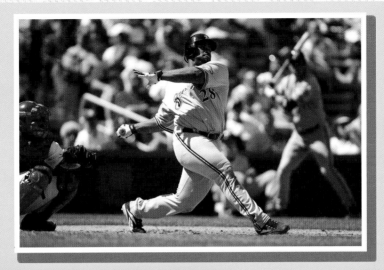

▲ Prince Fielder of
the '06 Brewers

The Minnesota Twins collected their
home runs against the Kansas City
Athletics. The Cincinnati Reds were
on the losing end in the other four
games. And that's a record in itself!

OUT OF THE PARK

Sixteen players in MLB history
have hit four home runs in a single
game. Hall of Famers Lou Gehrig,
Willie Mays, and Mike Schmidt each
achieved the feat. For two players,
Ed Delahanty and Bob Horner, four
home runs were not enough to win
the game. Their teams lost despite
the players' heroic hitting efforts.

▼ Mike Schmidt

CHAPTER 4

POSTSEASON and ALL-STARS

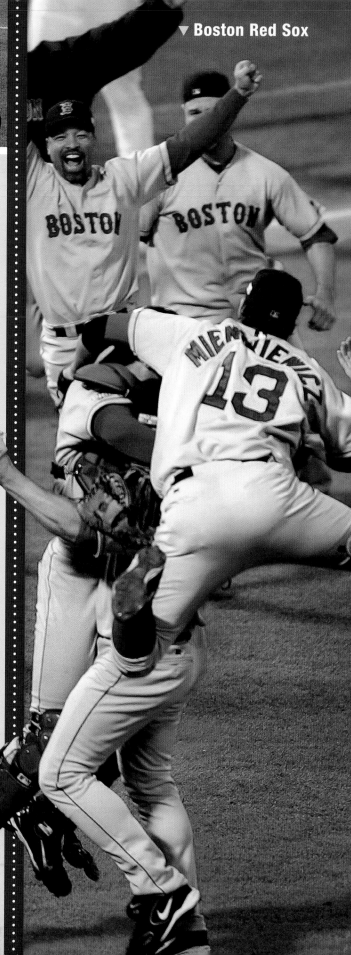

The Red Sox found themselves at the brink of elimination in the 2004 American League Championship Series. The New York Yankees had won the first three games, and no team in MLB history had come back after being down 0-3. New York was ahead 4-3 in the ninth inning of Game 4, when the Red Sox rallied against Yankees closer Mariano Rivera. They took Game 4, and went on to win the next three games and the ALCS. The Red Sox rode their momentum to a World Series win, sweeping the St. Louis Cardinals in four games, and ending an 86-year championship drought.

Since the modern era started in 1903, the World Series has pitted the best teams from the American League and National League against each other. Teams battle through the 162-game season for a spot in the playoffs. The St. Louis Cardinals added an 11th championship to their franchise history in 2011, but they have a long way to go to catch the Yankees.

MOST WORLD SERIES WINS (TEAM)

1.	New York Yankees	27
2.	St. Louis Cardinals	11
3.	Oakland Athletics	9
4.	Boston Red Sox	7
5.	Los Angeles Dodgers	6
	San Francisco Giants	6
7.	Cincinnati Reds	5
	Pittsburgh Pirates	5
9.	Detroit Tigers	4
10.	Four teams tied with	3

RECORD FACT The players with eight or more World Series wins earned all of their championship rings with the New York Yankees.

▼ New York Yankees

MOST WORLD SERIES CHAMPIONSHIPS (PLAYER)

1.	Yogi Berra	10
2.	Joe DiMaggio	9
3.	Bill Dickey	8
	Phil Rizzuto	8
	Frankie Crosetti	8
	Lou Gehrig	8
7.	Six players tied with	7

RECORD FACT Only three players have won the World Series MVP twice. They are Sandy Koufax, Bob Gibson, and Reggie Jackson.

▲ Yogi Berra

Hitting a home run to win the World Series is the dream of any player to pick up a baseball. But it has only happened twice in MLB history. Joe Carter of the Toronto Blue Jays came to the plate with his team trailing by one during Game 6 of the 1993 World Series. With two on and one out, he hit a series-winning homer to give the Jays their second straight championship. The only walk-off home run in Game 7 of the World Series belongs to Bill Mazeroski of the 1960 Pittsburgh Pirates. The Pirates second baseman led off the bottom of the ninth inning with the game tied 9-9. He drove the second pitch over the left-field wall, and the Pirates celebrated an upset over the New York Yankees.

▲ Joe Carter

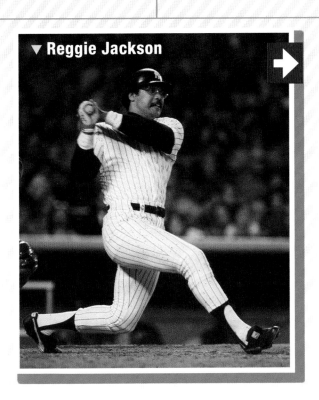

▼ Reggie Jackson

There is a good reason why Reggie Jackson is called Mr. October. He is known for his clutch hitting during the postseason, which helped him to five championship victories. His best performance was in Game 6 of the 1977 World Series. The New York Yankees led the series 3–2 against the Los Angeles Dodgers. Jackson hit home runs in three consecutive at bats, and the Yankees clinched the game and the series. His five home runs in the 1977 World Series have only been matched once. Philadelphia Phillies second baseman Chase Utley hit five homers in the 2009 World Series, but his Phillies still lost to the Yankees.

ALL STAR APPEARANCES

1.	Hank Aaron	21
2.	Willie Mays	20
	Stan Musial	20
4.	Cal Ripken Jr.	19
5.	Rod Carew	18
	Carl Yastrzemski	18
7.	Ted Williams	17
	Pete Rose	17
9.	Mickey Mantle	16
10.	Five players tied with	15

ALL-STAR MVPS

Considering the All-Star Game features the best players in baseball, it's quite an honor to be chosen as the All-Star MVP. The award goes to the top player of the game. Only four players have earned the award twice in their careers: Willie Mays, Steve Garvey, Gary Carter, and Cal Ripken Jr.

▲ Willie Mays

▼ Joe DiMaggio

CHAPTER 5

BALLPARK FAVORITES

Professional baseball is full of stats, records, and numbers. Sometimes the record is so amazing— or bizarre—that it holds a special place in baseball history.

Although many baseball records are impressive, there are some that are considered unbreakable. Whether the records were made through chance, determination, or a change in the way the game is played, they are considered near impossible to break. Joe DiMaggio's hitting streak is considered one of the unbreakable records in baseball. No player has come within 10 games of DiMaggio's record.

Like Joe DiMaggio, there are other players whose names have become famous for their incredible records. And although any record can be broken, a few may stand the test of time.

▲ **Cal Ripken Jr.**

▼ *Cal Ripken Jr.'s Iron Man Streak*
Cal Ripken Jr. took the field for a game against the Toronto Blue Jays May 30, 1982. Little did he know that the game would mark the beginning of a legendary streak. Starting with that game, Ripken played in 2,632 consecutive games spanning 17 seasons. He far surpassed Lou Gehrig's 59-year-old record of 2,130 games.

Why the record will be tough to break:
Players today rarely play every game in a season. Managers give their players off days to rest. On those days the players still wear their uniforms and watch the game from the dugout, but usually don't play.

▼ *Cy Young's 511 Wins*
You know you've had an impressive career when an award is named after you, and Cy Young is no exception. His most amazing stat is the 511 wins he earned during his career (1890–1911). He started a record 815 games and completed 749 of them—another record.

▼ **Cy Young**

Why the record will be tough to break:
Pitchers today are not expected to pitch in as many games or work through as many innings as pitchers did in Cy Young's era. When starting rotations became popular, pitchers were only expected to start every fourth or fifth game. That gave them fewer chances to earn wins. Plus, relief pitchers often take the reins late in games. The pitchers to come closest to Young's record within the last decade are Greg Maddux and Roger Clemens. They had 355 and 354 wins—not even close to Young's 511.

▼ Nolan Ryan

Nolan Ryan's Career Strikeouts

Nolan Ryan's 5,714 career strikeouts almost seems impossible. The "Express" mowed down batters over 27 seasons, averaging more than 200 strikeouts per season. He topped 300 strikeouts in six seasons, including an impressive 383 Ks in 1973.

Why the record will be tough to break:

The league leaders in strikeouts today tally more than 200 Ks in a season. But it's not too often that a player lasts 27 years in the majors—especially a pitcher. Plus, Ryan had six seasons of at least 250 innings pitched and a career total of 5,386 innings. Today's pitchers don't have as many opportunities to strike out batters. With 4,875 strikeouts, Randy Johnson came the closest to knocking Ryan off the throne. The next closest active pitcher, Javier Vazquez, has only half as many strikeouts as Ryan.

▼ Johnny Vander Meer

▼ *Johnny Vander Meer's Back-to-Back No-Hitters*

Cincinnati Reds pitcher Johnny Vander Meer wasted no time in jumping into the major league spotlight. In 1938, his first full season in the majors, he threw back-to-back no-hitters. He walked three and struck out four in the first game against the Boston Braves. The next game, which was against the Brooklyn Dodgers, was a little wild, with Vander Meer walking eight batters. Despite his lack of control, he didn't allow a single hit, and he remains the only pitcher to achieve the feat.

Why the record will be tough to break:

There have been more than 250 no-hitters in MLB history, so it's possible that a pitcher could repeat the record with back-to-back no-hitters. But to *break* the record, a pitcher would have to throw three straight no-hitters. Nolan Ryan had seven career no-hitters, but the closest two were two months apart.

▼ Alfonso Soriano

▼ The 40/40 Club

A player has to have power behind his swing to hit 40 home runs in a season. Similarly, a player needs to be quick on his feet to achieve 40 stolen bases. But it takes an unusual player to hit 40 home runs and steal 40 bases in one season. This elite 40/40 club is made up of only four players: Jose Canseco (1988), Barry Bonds (1996), Alex Rodriguez (1998), and Alfonso Soriano (2006). Amazingly, Soriano also had 41 doubles in 2006.

▼ Triple Crown

The triple crown is one of the rarest feats in baseball. Last achieved in 1967, the triple crown is awarded when a player leads or ties his league in home runs, RBIs, and batting average at the end of the season. Thirteen players have won the award. Hall of Famers Ted Williams and Rogers Hornsby accomplished the feat twice.

On the other side of the ball, there's also a triple crown for pitching. It's achieved if a pitcher ties or leads his league in wins, strikeouts, and earned run average at the end of the season. Three players have earned the triple crown three times: Walter Johnson of the Washington Senators, Grover Alexander of the Philadelphia Phillies and the Chicago Cubs, and Sandy Koufax of the Los Angeles Dodgers. In 2011 the Dodgers' Clayton Kershaw earned the National League pitching triple crown. Not to be outdone, the Detroit Tigers' Justin Verlander won the pitching triple crown in the American League.

The Cycle

If a player gets a single, double, triple, and home run in one game, it's called hitting for the cycle. More than 250 players have hit for the cycle. But only 14 have completed a natural cycle, which is collecting the hits in order (single, double, triple, home run). On May 7, 2008, Carlos Gomez of the Minnesota Twins became the fourth player to hit for the reverse natural cycle (home run, triple, double, single).

▼ Carlos Gomez

▼ Clayton Kershaw

Unassisted Triple Plays

A team can get out of a jam quickly if they can turn a triple play. On a rare occasion, it takes only one player to pull it off! Fifteen players have been at the right place at the right time and collected all three outs in a single play. It often happens on a hit-and-run, so the runners are on the move during the pitch. The batter hits a line drive up the middle, and either the second baseman or shortstop snags the ball in the air for the first out. Then he steps on second base for the force out and tags the runner heading to first for the third out. The Detroit Tigers' Johnny Neun and Philadelphia Phillies' Eric Bruntlett are the only players who have ended a game with a triple put out.

GOLD GLOVE LEADERS

Have you heard the expression that defense wins games? The players on the following lists took that advice to heart. They were exceptional at their positions and earned many Gold Glove awards during their careers.

CATCHER	
1. Ivan Rodriguez	13
2. Johnny Bench	10
3. Bob Boone	7
4. Jim Sundberg	6
5. Bill Freehan	5
6. Del Crandall	4
Charles Johnson	4
Mike Matheny	4
Yadier Molina	4*
Tony Pena	4

*Active player

▲ Ivan Rodriguez

PITCHER	
1. Greg Maddux	18
2. Jim Kaat	16
3. Bob Gibson	9
4. Bobby Shantz	8
5. Mark Langston	7
Mike Mussina	7
7. Ron Guidry	5
Phil Niekro	5
Kenny Rogers	5
10. Jim Palmer	4

▲ Greg Maddux

GOLD GLOVE LEADERS

FIRST BASE ||||||||||||||||||||||||

1.	Keith Hernandez	11
2.	Don Mattingly	9
3.	George Scott	8
4.	Vic Power	7
	Bill White	7
6.	Wes Parker	6
	J.T. Snow	6
8.	Steve Garvey	4
	Mark Grace	4
	Mark Teixeira	4*

*Active player

▲ Keith Hernandez

SECOND BASE ||||||||||||||||||||||

1.	Roberto Alomar	10
2.	Ryne Sandberg	9
3.	Bill Mazeroski	8
	Frank White	8
5.	Joe Morgann	5
	Bobby Richardson	5
7.	Craig Biggio	4
	Bret Boone	4
	Bobby Grich	4
	Orlando Hudson	4*

*Active player

▲ Roberto Alomar

GOLD GLOVE LEADERS

SHORTSTOP		
1.	Ozzie Smith	13
2.	Omar Vizquel	11
3.	Luis Aparicio	9
4.	Mark Belanger	8
5.	Dave Concepcion	5
	Derek Jeter	5*
7.	Tony Fernandez	4
	Alan Trammell	4
9.	Barry Larkin	3
	Roy McMillan	3
	Rey Ordonez	3
	Jimmy Rollins	3*

*Active player

▲ Ozzie Smith

THIRD BASE		
1.	Brooks Robinson	16
2.	Mike Schmidt	10
3.	Scott Rolen	8
4.	Buddy Bell	6
	Eric Chavez	6
	Robin Ventura	6
7.	Ken Boyer	5
	Doug Rader	5
	Ron Santo	5
10.	Gary Gaetti	4
	Matt Williams	4

▲ Brooks Robinson

OUTFIELD |||||||||||||||||||

1.	Roberto Clemente	12
	Willie Mays	12
3.	Ken Griffey Jr.	10
	Andruw Jones	10*
	Al Kaline	10
	Ichiro Suzuki	10*
7.	Torii Hunter	9*
8.	Paul Blair	8
	Barry Bonds	8
	Andre Dawson	8
	Jim Edmonds	8
	Dwight Evans	8
	Garry Maddox	8

*Active player

RECORD FACT

Each season MLB awards the title of Most Valuable Player to one player in the National League and one in the American League. Barry Bonds earned the award seven times in his career—four more than the next closest player.

▲ Willie Mays during the Giants' first game in San Francisco after moving from New York in 1958

▼ Tommy John

MOST SEASONS PLAYED ||||||||||||||||||||||||||||

1.	**Nolan Ryan**	27	Mets/Angels/Astros/ Rangers	1966, 1968–1993
	Cap Anson	27	Forest Citys/Athletics/ White Stockings/Colts	1871–1897
3.	**Deacon McGuire**	26	Blue Stockings/ Wolverines/Quakers/ Blues/Broncos/ Statesmen/Senators/ Superbas/Tigers/ Highlanders/ Americans/Naps	1884–1888, 1890–1908, 1910, 1912
	Tommy John	26	Indians/White Sox/ Dodgers/Yankees/ Angels/Athletics	1963–1974, 1976–1989
5.	**Eddie Collins**	25	Athletics/White Sox	1906–1930
	Rickey Henderson	25	Athletics/Yankees/ Blue Jays/Padres/ Angels/Mets/Mariners/ Red Sox/Dodgers	1979–2003
	Charlie Hough	25	Dodgers/Rangers/ White Sox/Marlins	1970–1994
	Jim Kaat	25	Senators/Twins/White Sox/Phillies/Yankees/ Cardinals	1959–1983
	Bobby Wallace	25	Spiders/Perfectos/ Browns/Cardinals	1894–1918
10.	**Many players tied with**	24		

A FIVE-DECADE RECORD

▼ **Minnie Minoso**

Minnie Minoso tied a major league record by playing in five decades. He started with the Indians in 1949 at age 23. He played from 1951 through 1964 for four teams, leading the league in triples twice and tying for the lead once. After a 12-year break, he returned to the White Sox for three games in 1976. In 1980, at age 54, he batted twice for the White Sox before ending his career.

Nick Altrock, who set the five-decade record, also played for the White Sox, pitching two complete games for the victorious Sox in the 1906 World Series. He joined the majors in 1898 and made his final plate appearance in 1933 for the Washington Senators, where he had been a coach since 1912.

RECORD FACT

Youngest Player: Ninth grader Joe Nuxhall pitched for the Cincinnati Reds in a 1944 game when he was 15 years, 10 months, 11 days old.

Oldest Player: Hall of Famer Satchel Paige pitched his last game in 1965 for the Kansas City Athletics when he was 59 years, 2 months, 18 days old.

LUCKY 13?

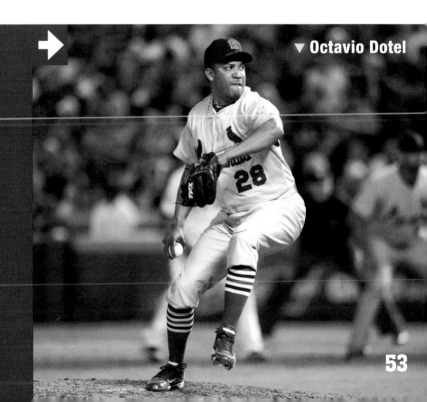

▼ **Octavio Dotel**

Some players stay with the same team for their entire careers. Other players find themselves in a new uniform every other season. Four players have spent time with 12 teams over their careers: Octavio Dotel, Mike Morgan, Matt Stairs, and Ron Villone. In 2012 Dotel set a record by playing for his 13th team, the Detroit Tigers.

▼ Tony LaRussa

CAREER WINS BY A MANAGER ||||||||||||||||||||||||||||

1.	Connie Mack	3,731	Pirates/Athletics	1894–1896, 1901–1950
2.	John McGraw	2,763	Orioles/Giants	1899, 1901–1932
3.	Tony LaRussa	2,728	White Sox/ Athletics/Cardinals	1979–2011
4.	Bobby Cox	2,504	Braves/Blue Jays	1978–1985, 1990–2010
5.	Joe Torre	2,326	Mets/Braves/ Cardinals/Yankees/ Dodgers	1977–1984, 1990–2010
6.	Sparky Anderson	2,194	Reds/Tigers	1970–1995
7.	Bucky Harris	2,158	Senators/Tigers/ Red Sox/Phillies/ Yankees	1924–1943, 1947–1948, 1950–1956
8.	Joe McCarthy	2,125	Cubs/Yankees/ Red Sox	1926–1946, 1948–1950
9.	Walter Alston	2,040	Dodgers	1954–1976
10.	Leo Durocher	2,008	Dodgers/Giants/ Cubs/Astros	1939–1946, 1948–1955, 1966–1973

▼ Connie Mack

WIN SOME, LOSE SOME

Connie Mack tops the wins list, but he also tops the list of all-time losses by a manager with 3,948. Next in line is Tony LaRussa, but he has about 1,500 fewer losses than Mack.

And speaking of winners, Casey Stengel led the New York Yankees to five straight World Series victories from 1949 to 1953.

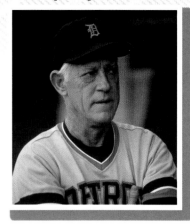

WORLD SERIES CHAMPIONSHIPS BY A MANAGER |||||		
1.	**Joe McCarthy**	7	Cubs/Yankees/Red Sox	1926–1946, 1948–1950
	Casey Stengel	7	Dodgers/Bees/ Braves/Yankees/Mets	1934–1936, 1938–1943, 1949–1960, 1962–1965
3.	**Connie Mack**	5	Pirates/Athletics	1894–1896, 1901–1950
4.	**Walter Alston**	4	Dodgers	1954–1976
	Joe Torre	4	Mets/Braves/ Cardinals/Yankees/ Dodgers	1977–1984, 1990–2010
6.	**Sparky Anderson**	3	Reds/Tigers	1970–1995
	Miller Huggins	3	Cardinals/Yankees	1913–1929
	Tony LaRussa	3	White Sox/Athletics/ Cardinals	1979–2011
	John McGraw	3	Orioles/Giants	1899, 1901–1932
10.	**Many managers tied with**	2		

![RECORD **FACT**]

Bobby Cox of the Atlanta Braves is the only manager to get ejected twice in the World Series. The first happened in 1992 during an argument over a check swing call. The second happened in 1996 when he disagreed with a called out of a baserunner attempting to steal.

THE BEST OF THE WORST

Some players earn records they'd rather not have. They can only hope that another player will come along who will take the title of "the best of the worst."

	CAREER STRIKEOUTS			
1.	Reggie Jackson	2,597	Athletics/Orioles/Yankees/Angels	1967–1987
2.	Jim Thome	2,487	Indians/Phillies/White Sox/Dodgers/Twins	1991–2011*
3.	Sammy Sosa	2,306	Rangers/White Sox/Cubs/Orioles	1989–2005, 2007
4.	Andres Galarraga	2,003	Expos/Cardinals/Rockies/Braves/Rangers/Giants/Expos/Angels	1985–1998, 2000–2004
5.	Jose Canseco	1,942	Athletics/Rangers/Red Sox/Blue Jays/Devil Rays/Yankees/White Sox	1985–2001
6.	Willie Stargell	1,936	Pirates	1962–1982
7.	Alex Rodriguez	1,916	Mariners/Rangers/Yankees	1994–2011*
8.	Mike Cameron	1,901	White Sox/Reds/Mariners/Mets/Padres/Brewers/Red Sox/Marlins	1995–2011*
9.	Mike Schmidt	1,883	Phillies	1972–1989
10.	Fred McGriff	1,882	Blue Jays/Padres/Braves/Devil Rays/Cubs/Dodgers	1986–2004

*Active player

THE BEST OF THE WORST

▼ Drew Stubbs

SINGLE SEASON STRIKEOUTS				
1.	Mark Reynolds	223	Diamondbacks	2009
2.	Mark Reynolds	211	Diamondbacks	2010
3.	Drew Stubbs	205	Reds	2011
4.	Mark Reynolds	204	Diamondbacks	2008
5.	Adam Dunn	199	Nationals	2010
	Ryan Howard	199	Phillies	2007
	Ryan Howard	199	Phillies	2008
8.	Jack Cust	197	Athletics	2008
9.	Mark Reynolds	196	Orioles	2011
10.	Adam Dunn	195	Reds	2004

RECORD FACT Eight players have struck out six times in one game. Alex Gonzalez of the Toronto Blue Jays is the only one of them to strike out during every plate appearance.

SWINGING FOR THE FENCES

In only five years in the majors, Mark Reynolds has hit 158 home runs, averaging about 32 per season. But with the big swings come big misses. In four of his five seasons, Reynolds has landed in the top 10 for single-season strikeouts. With 963 strikeouts through 2011, Reynolds may find himself in the top 10 career strikeouts list before long.

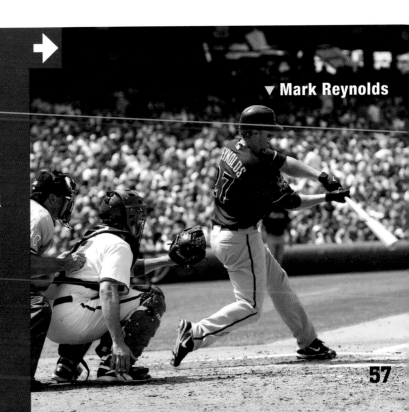

▼ Mark Reynolds

THE BEST OF THE WORST

1.	Herman Long	1,096	Cowboys/Beaneaters/Highlanders/Tigers/Phillies	1889–1904
2.	Bill Dahlen	1,080	Colts/Orphans/Superbas/Giants/Doves/Dodgers	1891–1911
3.	Deacon White	1,018	Forest Cities/Red Stockings/White Stockings/Reds/Bisons/Wolverines/Alleghenys	1871–1890
4.	Germany Smith	1,009	Mountain City/Blues/Grays/Reds/Bridegrooms/Browns	1884–1898
5.	Tommy Corcoran	992	Burghers/Athletics/Grooms/Bridegrooms/Reds/Giants	1890–1907
6.	Fred Pfeffer	980	Trojans/White Stockings/Pirates/Colonels/Giants/Colts	1882–1897
7.	Cap Anson	976	Forest Citys/Athletics/White Stockings/Colts	1871–1897
8.	Monte Ward	952	Grays/Gothams/Giants/Ward's Wonders/Grooms	1878–1894
9.	Jack Glasscock	895	Blues/Outlaw Reds/Maroons/Hoosiers/Giants/Browns/Pirates/Colonels/Senators	1879–1895
10.	Ed McKean	892	Blues/Spiders/Perfectos	1887–1899

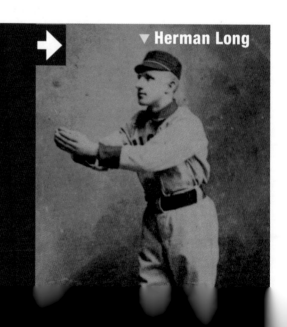

▼ Herman Long

ERROR UPON ERROR

In 1889 Herman Long of the Kansas City Cowboys committed 122 errors in 137 games. The Philadelphia Athletics' Billy Shindle was even worse in 1890 if you consider the number of games played. He committed 122 errors in 132 games. Andy Leonard of the Boston Red Stockings didn't have many career errors, but he had one of the worst outings of any fielder in MLB history. He committed nine

CAREER HIT BATTERS

1.	Gus Weyhing	277	Athletics/Ward's Wonders/Phillies/Pirates/Colonels/Senators/Cardinals/Superbas/Reds/Blues	1887–1896, 1898–1901
2.	Chick Fraser	219	Colonels/Spiders/Phillies/Athletics/Beaneaters/Reds/Cubs	1896–1909
3.	Pink Hawley	210	Browns/Pirates/Reds/Giants/Brewers	1892–1901
4.	Walter Johnson	205	Senators	1907–1927
5.	Randy Johnson	190	Expos/Mariners/Astros/Diamondbacks/Yankees/Giants	1988–2009
	Eddie Plank	190	Athletics/Terriers/Browns	1901–1917
7.	Tim Wakefield	186	Pirates/Red Sox	1992–1993, 1995–2011
8.	Tony Mullane	185	Wolverines/Eclipse/Browns/Blue Stockings/Red Stockings/Orioles/Spiders	1881–1884, 1886–1894
9.	Joe McGinnity	179	Orioles/Superbas/Giants	1899–1908
10.	Charlie Hough	174	Dodgers/Rangers/White Sox/Marlins	1970–1994

RECORD FACT

It's no wonder Tim Wakefield is in the top 10 for career hit batters. Wakefield is well-known for his knuckleball, a pitch with movement that is tough to predict—for the hitter, pitcher, *and* catcher.

BACK-TO-BACK-TO-BACK-TO-BACK

Only three pitchers have given up four home runs in a row. The Los Angeles Angels' Paul Foytack gave up four consecutive bombs against the Cleveland Indians in 1963. New York Yankees pitcher Chase Wright suffered the same fate in 2007 at the hands of the rival Boston Red Sox. Dave Bush of the Milwaukee Brewers was taken deep four times in a row by the Arizona Diamondbacks in 2010. Teams have hit four straight home runs on four other occasions, but they were against multiple pitchers.

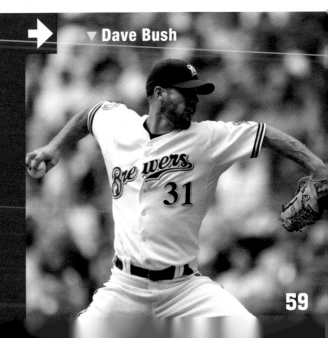
▼ Dave Bush

▼ Tony Mullane

		CAREER		
1.	Tony Mullane	343	Wolverines/Eclipse/Browns/Blue Stockings/Red Stockings/Orioles/Spiders	1881–1884, 1886–1894
2.	Nolan Ryan	277	Mets/Angels/Astros/Rangers	1966, 1968–1993
3.	Mickey Welch	274	Trojans/Gothams/Giants	1881–1892
4.	Bobby Mathews	253	Kekiongas/Canaries/Mutuals/Reds/Grays/Red Stockings/Athletics	1871–1877, 1879, 1881–1887
5.	Tim Keefe	240	Trojans/Metropolitans/Giants/Phillies	1880–1993
	Gus Weyhing	240	Athletics/Ward's Wonders/Phillies/Pirates/Colonels/Senators/Cardinals/Superbas/Reds	1887–1896, 1898–1901
7.	Phil Niekro	226	Braves/Yankees/Indians/Blue Jays	1965–1987
8.	Mark Baldwin	221	White Stockings/Solons/Pirates/Giants	1887–1893
	Pud Galvin	221	Brown Stockings/Bisons/Alleghenys/Burghers/Pirates/Browns	1875, 1879–1892
	Will White	221	Red Stockings/Reds/Wolverines	1877–1886

WILD PITCHES

▼ Matt Kilroy

SINGLE SEASON				
1.	Mark Baldwin	83	Solons	1889
2.	Tony Mullane	63	Blue Stockings	1884
	Bill Stemmyer	63	Beaneaters	1886
4.	Mike Morrison	62	Blues	1887
5.	Matt Kilroy	61	Orioles	1886
6.	Ed Seward	58	Athletics	1887
7.	Jersey Bakley	56	Keystones/Quicksteps/Cowboys	1884
	Gus Weyhing	56	Athletics	1888
9.	Ed Seward	54	Athletics	1888
10.	Tony Mullane	53	Red Stockings	1886

▼ J.R. Richard

REALLY, REALLY WILD

Three pitchers have had six wild pitches in a single game: Phil Niekro of the Atlanta Braves, J.R. Richard of the Houston Astros, and Bill Gullickson of the Montreal Expos. During an 1890 game, Bert Cunningham of the Buffalo Bisons threw five wild pitches in a single inning.

61

READ MORE

Berman, Len. *The Greatest Moments in Sports*.
Naperville, Ill.: Sourcebooks, 2009.

Fischer, David. *Babe Ruth: Legendary Slugger*.
New York: Sterling Publishing, 2010.

Jacobs, Greg. *The Everything Kids' Baseball Book: From Baseball History to Player Stats—With Lots of Homerun Fun in Between!*
Avon, Mass.: Adams Media, 2010.

LeBoutillier, Nate. *The Best of Everything Baseball Book*.
Mankato, Minn.: Capstone Press, 2011.

INTERNET SITES

FactHound offers a safe, fun way to find Internet sites related to this book. All of the sites on FactHound have been researched by our staff.

Here's all you do:

Visit *www.facthound.com*

Type in this code: 9781429687140

INDEX